I imagine

A Child's Book of Prayers

Rachel Rivett ✦ Mique Moriuchi

LION
CHILDREN'S

Contents

Every day I ask Our Father of All, our Lord
of Love, to help me; and every day he answers.
He shows me the beautiful green earth.
"Look!" he says. "Listen!"

If I open my eyes and ears, my heart and mind,
the earth opens like a book and I can read the
wisdom there, and imagine…

O Lord, if the sun is shining golden bright,

I imagine my heart is a beautiful flower

opening in your warmth and light and love.

O Lord, if things are hard, I imagine I'm a river
and you help me flow quick and clean
around the rocks that block my path.

O Lord, if it's winter dark, I light a candle and imagine your flame of love burning in my heart.

O Lord, if life is
stormy, I imagine I'm a tree,
tossed and tumbled in the wind,

and you show me how

my roots are growing stronger.

O Lord, if I'm full of joy, I imagine I'm a robin

singing sweet songs for everyone to hear.

O Lord, if I'm sad, I imagine I'm a seed curled up close in the arms of the earth and know that soon the sun will come out to warm me.

O Lord, if I'm too shy to ask for help,
I imagine I'm the moon and you're the sun

and feel how gladly you share your light with
so I too can shine upon the world.

O Lord, if I'm full of energy,

I run outside and imagine I'm a wild, whirling leaf

spinning in a breathless, blustery dance.

O Lord, if I feel like giving up, I imagine I'm an oak tree;
though my branches twist and turn and change direction,

m growing ever closer to your sky.

O Lord, if I'm worried,
I imagine I'm a baby bird about to fly.
I feel I'm on my own with nothing underneath me,

but when I spread my wings and leap,

you breathe the wind that catches me and carries me and lifts me so high.

O Lord, if I'm tired from too much thinking,
I imagine I'm the sky:

clear and bright and empty.

O Lord, if it's time to sleep, I imagine I'm the sea,

and my breath sings in-and-out, in-and-out:

an endless song of praises falling on your shore.